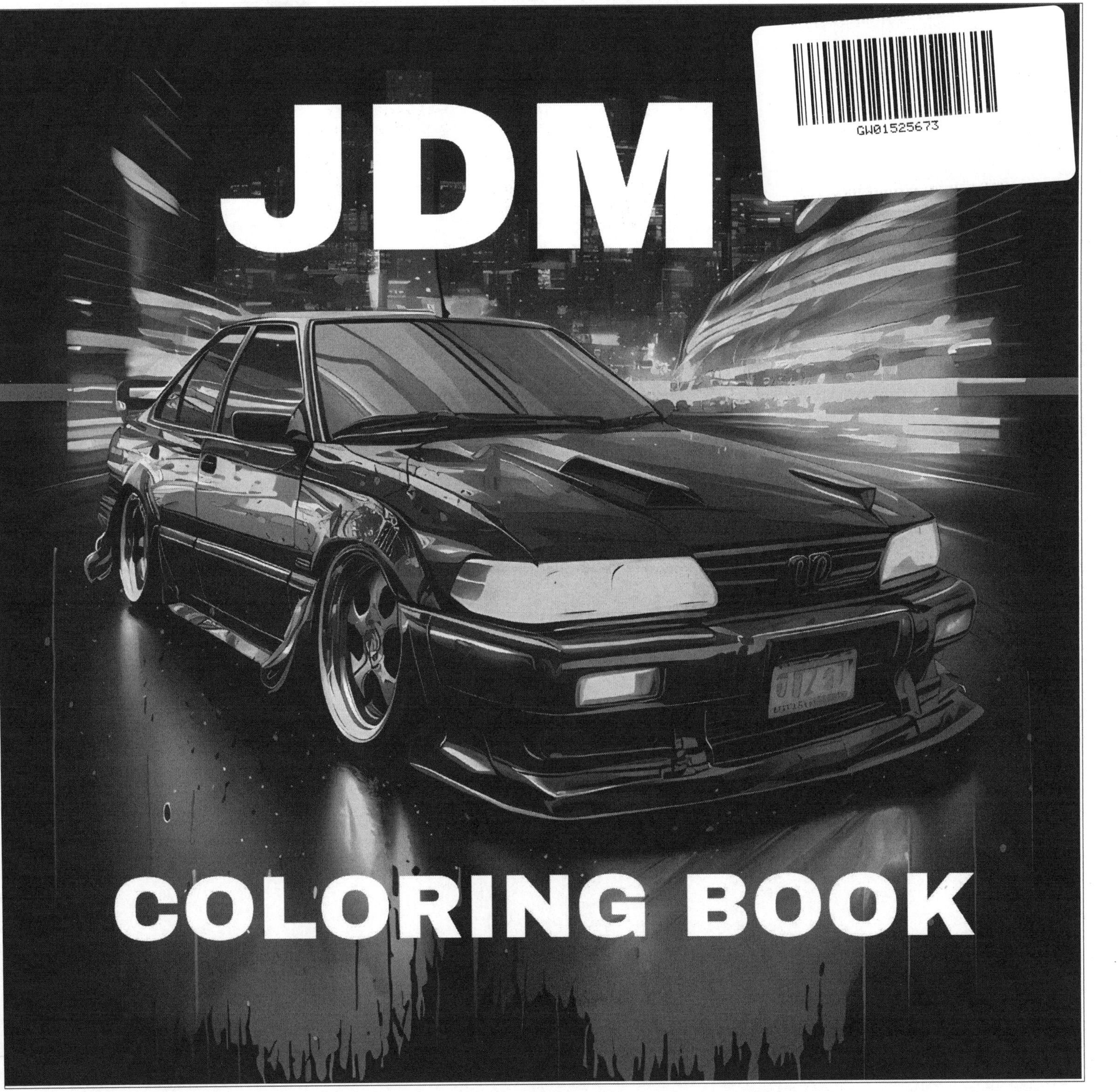
JDM
COLORING BOOK

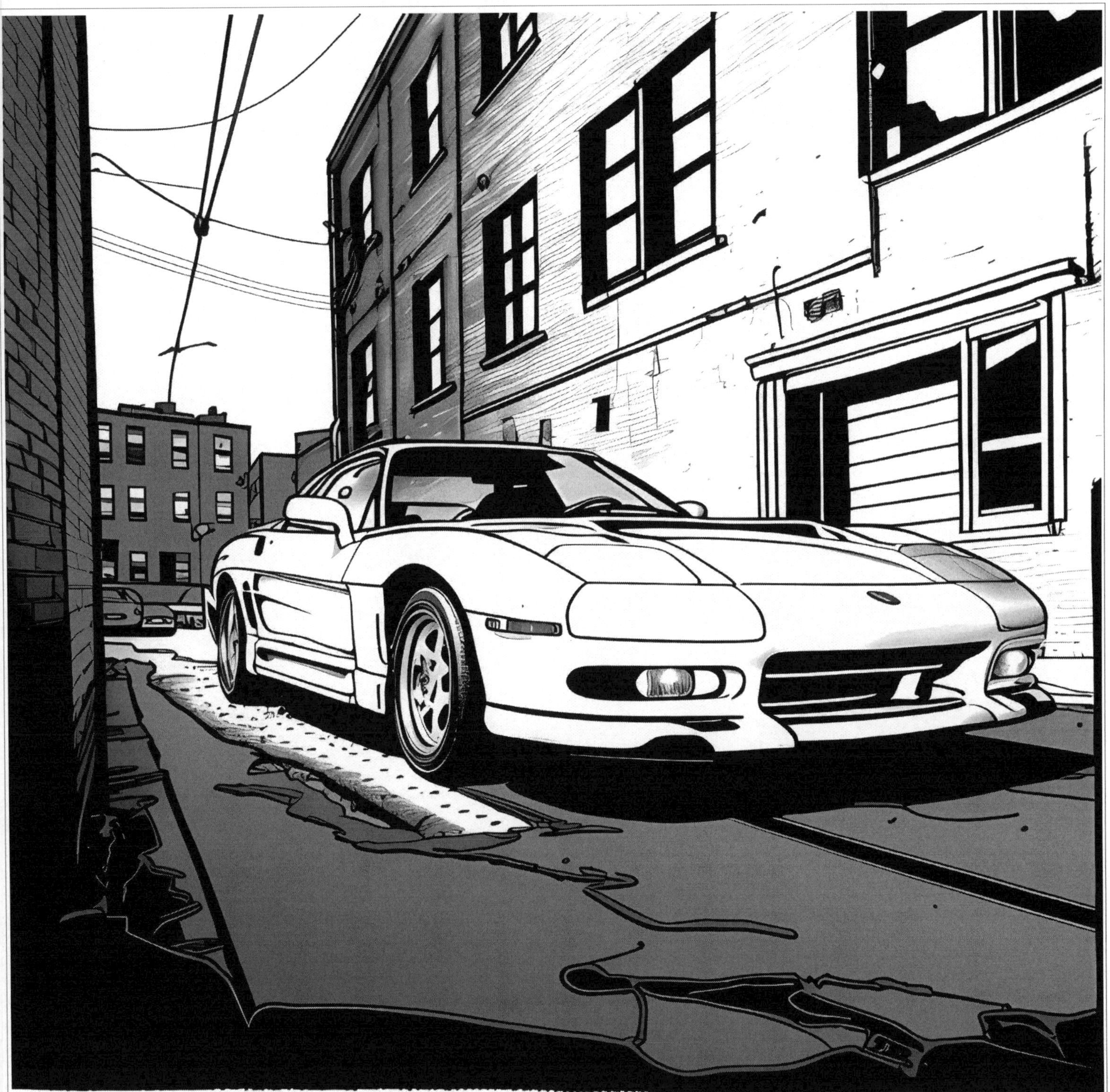

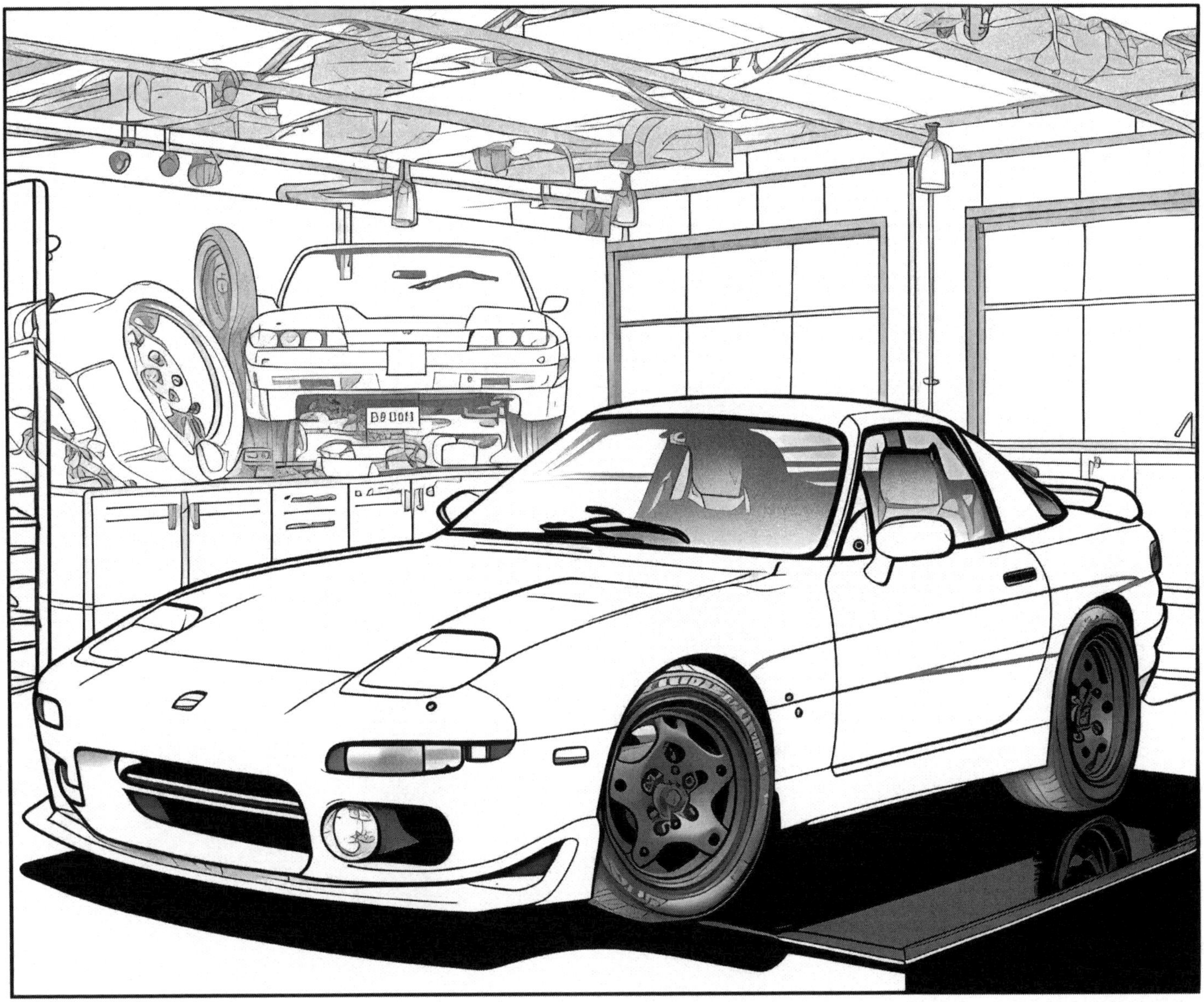

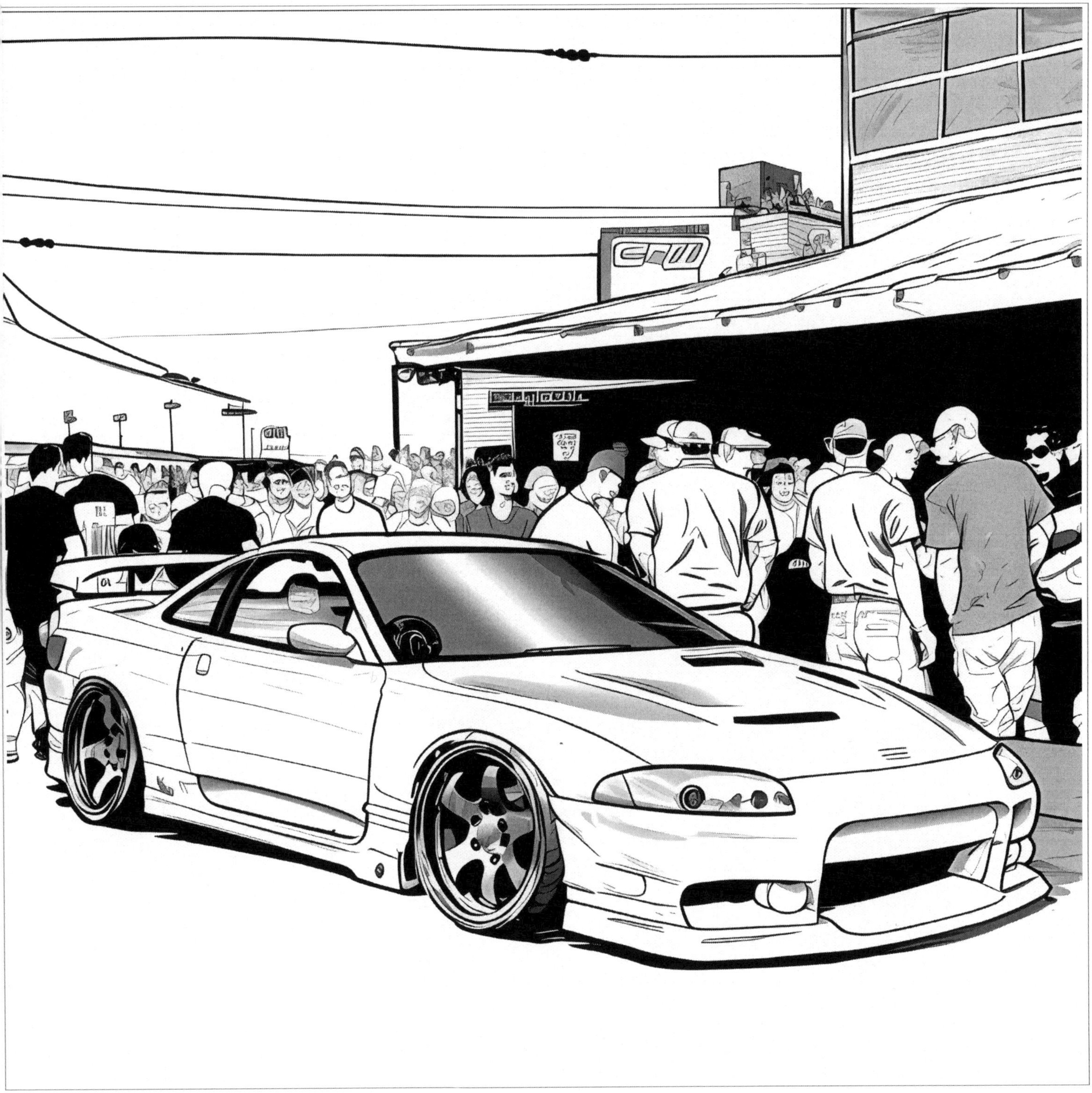

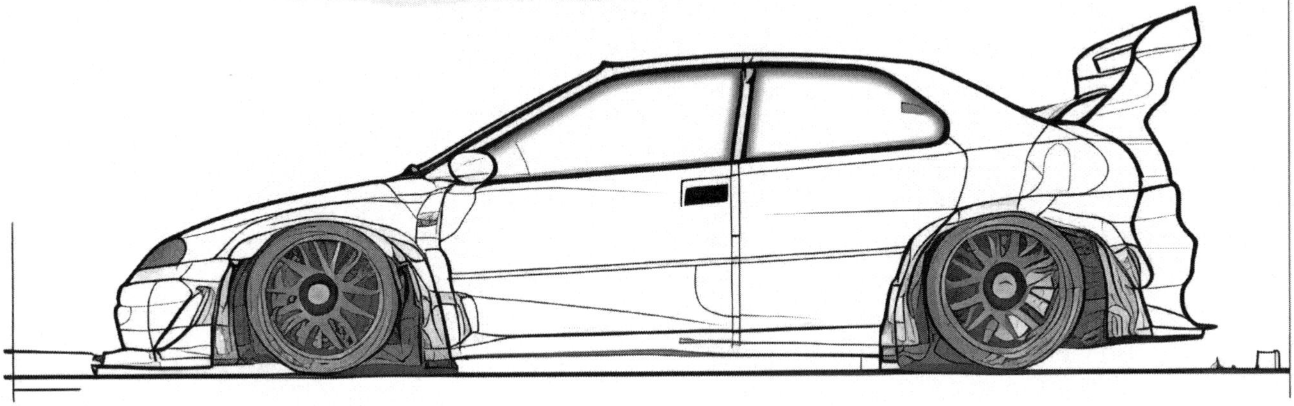

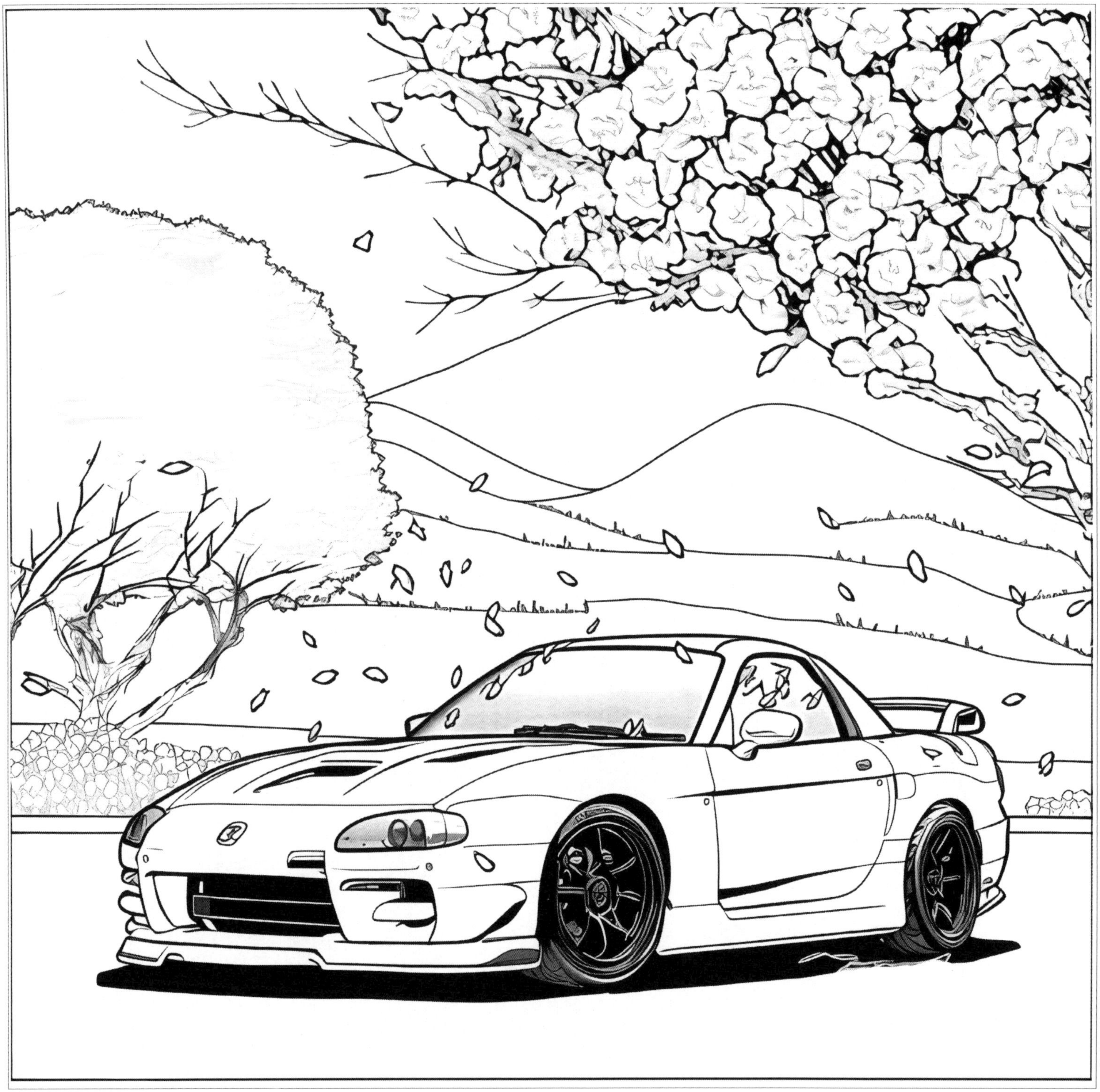

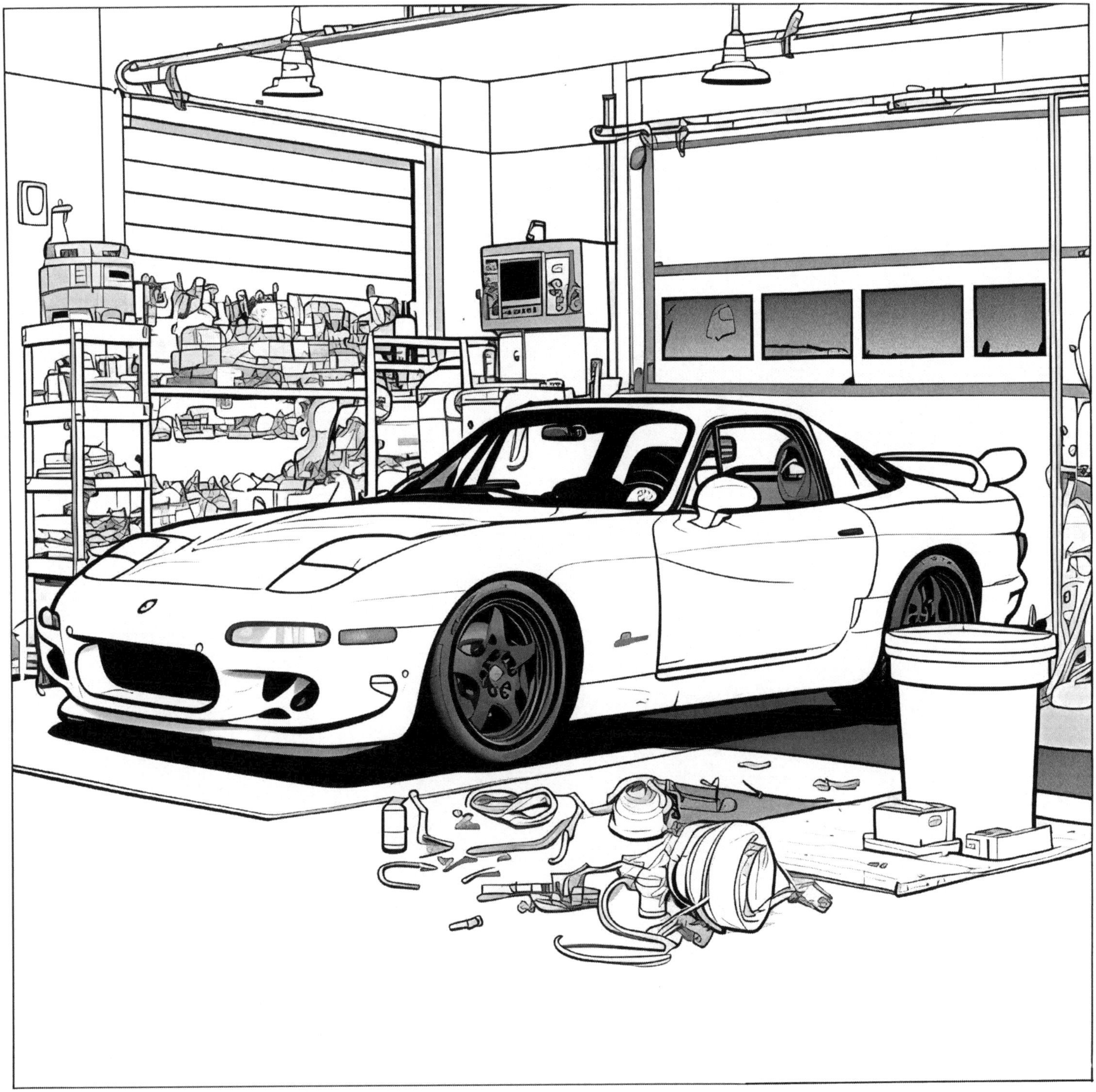

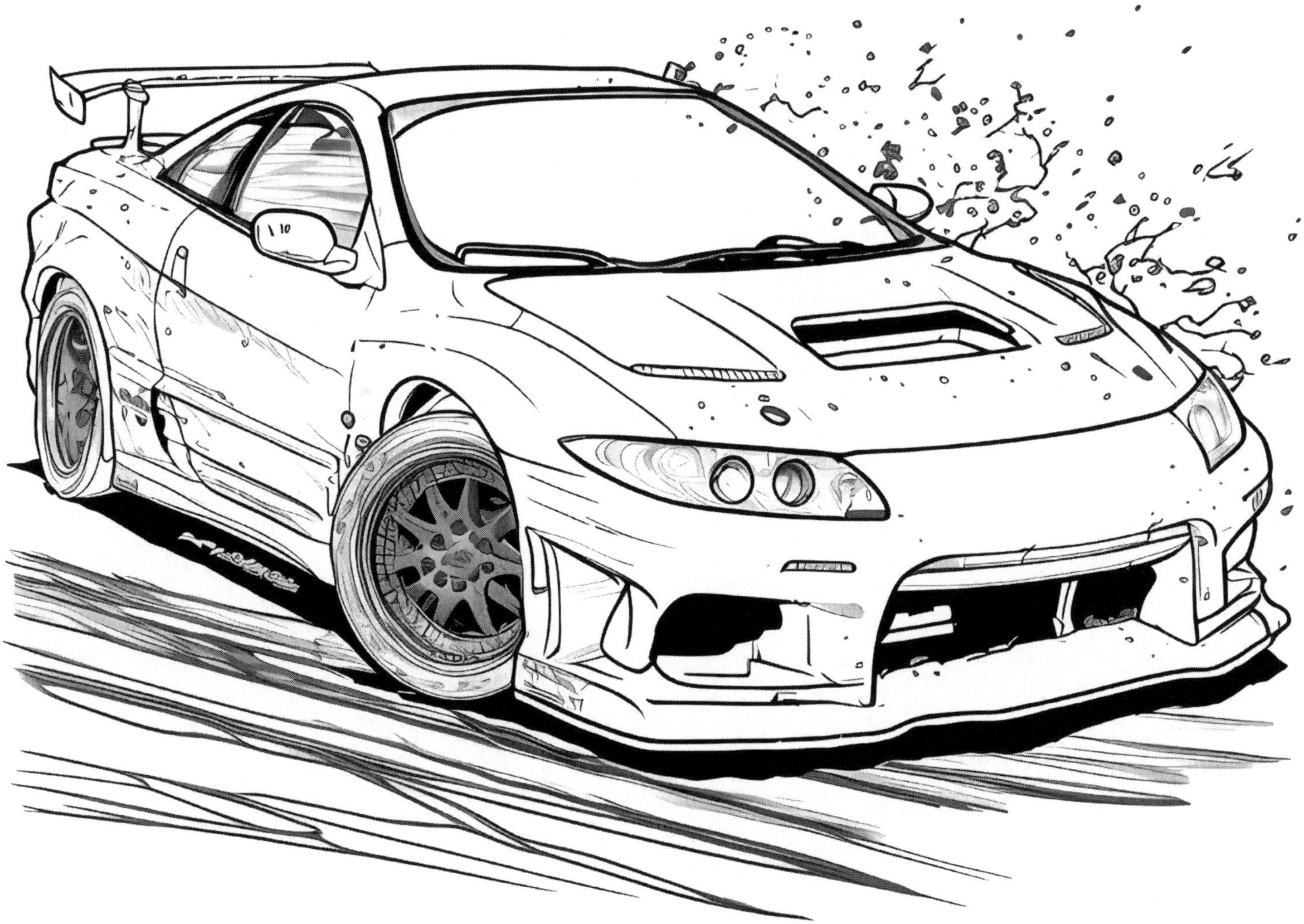

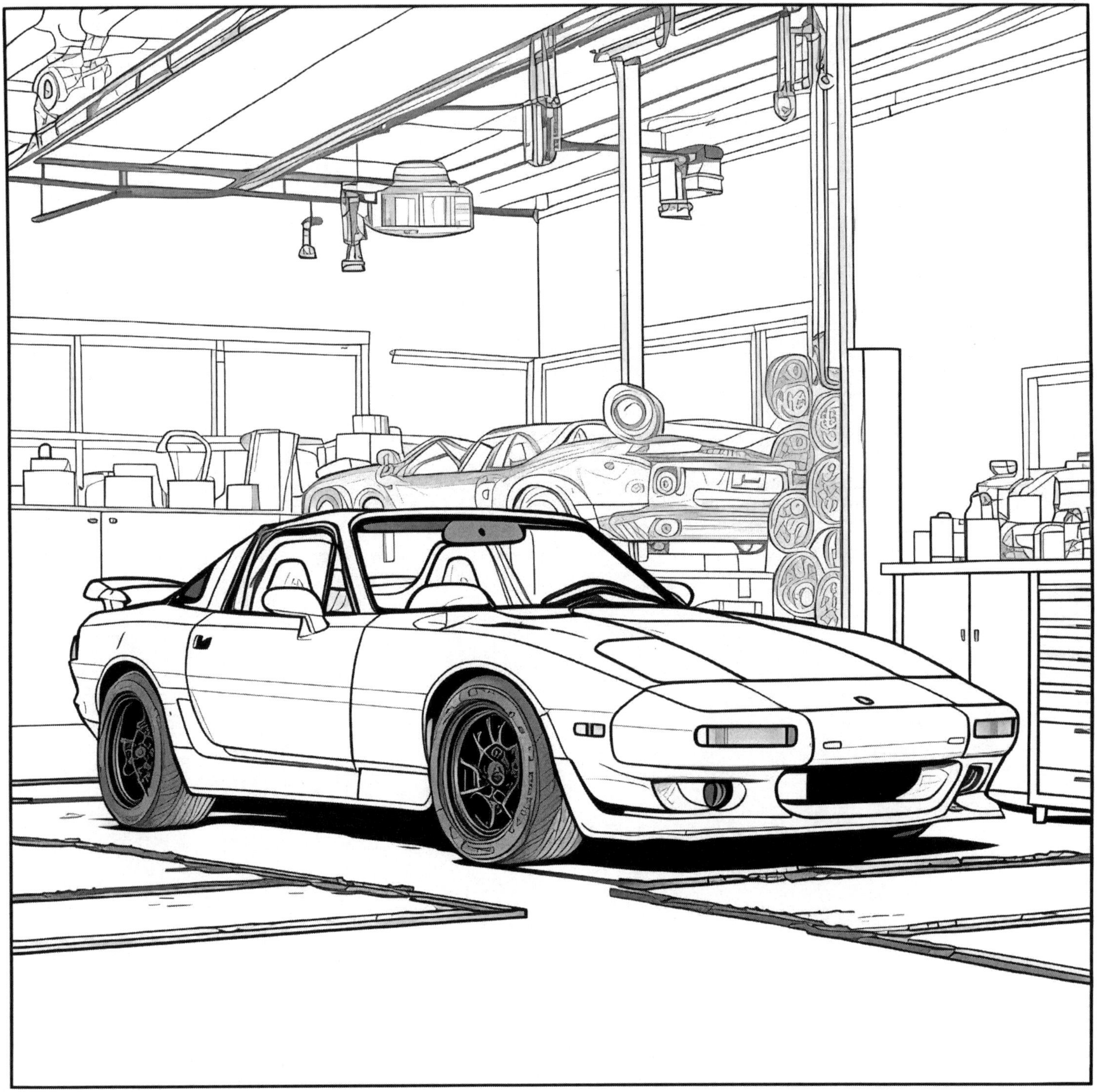

17

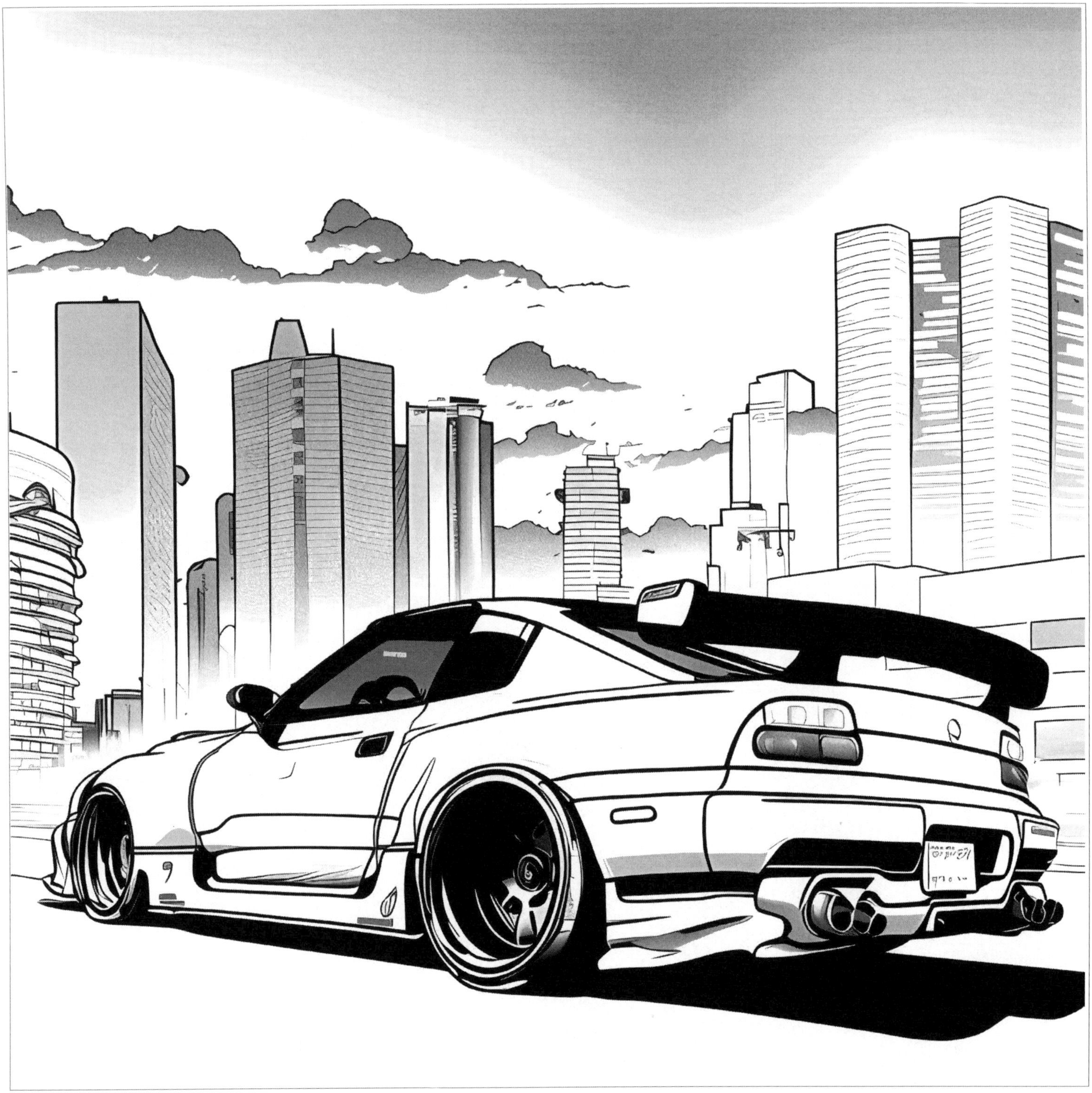

Printed in Great Britain
by Amazon

34347537R00059